A Cree Life

A Cree Life
The Art of Allen Sapp

Introduction by John Anson Warner
& Thecla Bradshaw

Allen Sapp

J. J. Douglas Ltd., Vancouver

J. J. Douglas Ltd.
1875 Welch Street
North Vancouver
British Columbia

Canadian Cataloguing in Publication Data

Sapp, Allen, 1929 —
 A Cree Life

  Bibliography: p.
  ISBN 0-88894-149-8

  1. Sapp, Allen, 1929 —   2. Cree
Indians.   3. Cree Indians – Art.   4. Cree
Indians – Biography.   I. Warner, John
Anson.   II. Bradshaw, Thecla.   III. Title.
ND249.S26A3   970'.004'97   C77-002173-5

Printed and bound in Canada

Acknowledgements

We extend sincere thanks to the following:
The Canada Council, Explorations Division;
President's Research Fund of the University of Regina;
Prof. Margaret A. Caron of Marianopolis College, Montreal;
John Forsyth; Julius Friesen; Gerry Hammersmith; Richard Holden;
Raymond Hull; Prof. Kurt Jonassohn of Concordia University, Montreal;
Gontran Laviolette; Nancy Neil Noonan; Sandra Semchuk;
Wilfred Tootoosis; Lorne Watson; Allen Willows; Loreen Wilsden.

Foreword

The purpose of this book is to provide insight into the life, nature and artistry of the Plains Cree artist Kiskayetum Saposkum, or Allen Sapp, as he is better known. Over fifty major exhibitions of Allen Sapp paintings in the nine-year period 1968-77 affirm an extraordinary public interest in his work, and we are well aware that owners of Sapp canvases and his many admirers wish to know more about the man himself. We have not written an art commentary, as Allen is only in mid-career and this would be premature, even presumptuous. Instead, we have written about the central features of his life to explain how he developed from a talented amateur into a professional artist of international renown. We could not do this without describing something of the history and culture of his Cree people. His paintings speak for themselves–just as they do for thousands of his admirers–but we have included some of Allen Sapp's comments with his paintings where we felt them to be appropriate and helpful.

We caution the reader that dates and places given in the text are often approximate. Old church and official records contain errors and contradictions, and sometimes the Indian people themselves do not agree in their recollections.

With charm and disarming simplicity, the Sapp paintings tell the universal story of people on the land. It is hoped that *A Cree Life* will bring honour to the gifted artist and his people as his paintings themselves have done, and that the thousands who are drawn to his exhibitions will have a beautiful record that captures the elusive magic of Kiskayetum's paintings.

Allen Sapp's People-The Cree

Saskatchewan is a Canadian province with considerable diversity in its terrain. Between the vast, undulating prairie to the south and the nearly impenetrable wilderness of the great Canadian Shield country to the north, there is a belt of parklands. This parkland area, with its subtle beauty of gently rolling hills and sporadic bush, is home for many of Saskatchewan's native Indians. It is peppered with the small reserves that are the treaty lands of the Plains Cree, Saulteaux and Assiniboine peoples. Here live the descendants of once mighty tribes who, during the eighteenth and nineteenth centuries, rode the prairie hunting buffalo and enjoying the free life of a nomadic people. They contributed more than their share of romance and colour to Canadian history.

The Cree were not originally indigenous to the Canadian plains but were a woodlands dwelling people. Before the advent of the white man, they lived in the region of the Canadian Shield between Hudson's Bay and Lake Winnipeg. Here, as a people of the forest, lakes and streams, they lived by hunting, fishing and gathering. When the white man established first contacts with them, in the period 1640 to 1690, they were a nomadic people of fierce and proud warriors. From 1690 to 1740, the Cree were involved in the fur trade and often served as middlemen between the English and French fur traders and the tribes deeper in the hinterland of Canada. As the demand for fur pelts grew, the Cree expanded westward in search of new areas for trapping and trade. By the latter portions of the eighteenth century, they occupied northern trapping areas across the present-day provinces of Manitoba, Saskatchewan, and Alberta.

In the early 1780s, terrible epidemics of the white man's disease, smallpox, decimated Cree numbers and this halted their westward expansion throughout Alberta. They became interested in the plains area south of the trapping region, for here were immense herds of buffalo which could provide a seemingly inexhaustible supply of food-both for their own consumption and for trading to fur posts in the north. It was also, at least at that time, a more healthy environment. From 1790 to 1820, many Cree bands moved onto the Saskatchewan plains for a summer of buffalo hunting and in the winter, they retreated into the parklands area to be better sheltered by the bush from the drifting snow. This alternation of seasons between parklands and the plains proved a wise strategy for the Cree.

From 1820 to 1880, the Western Cree became a classic buffalo hunting people: a mounted nomadic people cleverly using the buffalo to provide most of their needs. These bands of Cree became so different from their woodlands cousins that they became known as the Plains Cree. One of these Plains Cree bands in the 1870s was headed by a distinguished warrior, Red Pheasant, after whom his band was named.

In the 1870s, Sir John A. Macdonald's government of the newly founded

Dominion of Canada, required the plains region for a railroad, and for farms, towns, and cities, and persuaded the Indian leaders of Saskatchewan to surrender their rights to exclusive domicile on the prairie. In return, the government promised them reserves for "as long as the rivers flow, the grasses grow." They also promised them aid in health, education, food rations, agricultural implements, and the means of learning a new way of life. As was so often true, the white man was better at making promises than in keeping them.

Several of the bands-called the River Cree-liked the Battle River area and chose it for their reserves. To the immediate south of North Battleford are the Eagle Hills which is a region of gently rolling prairie and thick parkland bush. It was here that Chief Red Pheasant located his reserve.

By 1878, the northern buffalo herd was on the verge of extinction and the Cree had no other choice than to move on to the reserves, where they were confined in small areas and reduced to the status of sedentary paupers, dependent upon the generosity of the federal government and missionary groups, or on what they could scrape together themselves. The government promises were not kept and the Cree were soon in a state of semi-starvation. Robert Jefferson, first schoolteacher on the Red Pheasant reserve, has penned this description of the plight of the Cree during this dark period in his *Fifty Years on the Saskatchewan:*

> In the spring of 1879, our Indians received the 'assistance' cited in the treaty, viz: four oxen, six cows, two plows, with spades, hoes and a few garden seeds . . . the attempt they made was, even to a considerate eye, absolutely ludicrous. While one held the plow handles and a second sat on the beam, each ox had a driver by its side. The oxen were freight animals and plowing, or working at anything in pairs was new to them, as to the men.
>
> The piece of ground was plentifully covered with short brush and the roots kept pushing the share out of the ground . . . But the plowing was at length finished and the grain sown. At the fencing, the women, who were quite handy with the axe, ably supplemented the efforts and sustained the reputation of the band in their essay at agriculture.
>
> The women also put in the garden seeds after rooting up the ground with grub hoes. One by one they would drop the tiny seeds with as much care as though they were sowing grains of gold . . .
>
> There was more rain than usual that year and flies were proportionately numerous and vicious . . . With government scythes they tried hay-making, but proved too new to the job.
>
> Their little crop came to nothing, and the winter played havoc with their cattle. It was starvation. . . .

From the 1880s until the end of World War II, the Cree struggled with poverty. Apart from their contacts with neighbouring townspeople and white settlers (who had none too easy a life themselves), the Cree dealt mainly with such white authority figures as the government agent, missionaries, school teachers and the para-military Royal Canadian Mounted Police.

The Cree were left largely to fend for themselves as Government rations and provisions were never enough to assure even survival. They hunted game such as rabbits, deer, prairie chickens, ducks, and geese and were often reduced to eating gophers. The women gathered edible roots, wild fruit and natural vegetation to supplement the diet. After they were introduced to the white man's flour, a bread-like bannock was baked which today is the mainstay of the Cree diet.

Eventually, a few of the Cree learned animal husbandry and farming techniques well enough to become relatively prosperous. Sometimes younger Cree men would leave the reserve for employment in the white world as cowboys on local ranches or to work on threshing crews in the fall harvest season. On the reserve itself, some cut wood in the bush to sell to the white townspeople for fence pickets or as fuel for their stoves.

But at its best, life was never easy for the Cree of the Eagle Hills. Their way of life as a nomadic, hunting people was over and they found it hard to adjust to new ways. It was not uncommon for a Cree man to disdain becoming a farmer, since his traditional role had been that of a hunter and warrior. Even if all the Cree men had tried to become good farmers, the reserves were too small and the land too poor to sustain them.

As if poverty were not enough, there were the twin scourges of disease and alcohol. In the early days of white contact there were dreadful epidemics of small pox, measles, whooping cough, and pneumonia. During the reserve days of the first half of the twentieth century, tuberculosis was a common and deadly affliction. Tables of statistics are unnecessary to illustrate the point: of the nine people in the Sapp family, five died from tuberculosis. While tuberculosis is now under control, alcoholism remains a serious problem.

Despite their difficulties, the Cree never lost their sense of themselves as a people and have retained much of their traditional culture. And although much has been lost or made irrelevant in their lives, they are still Naheyow (the people) and many have clung to their native religion. Extended family units and kinship ties remained strong and warm.

Not even the outlawing by Sir John A. Macdonald's government in 1885 of the Sun Dance destroyed their religion; their observance of this most sacred of religious rituals simply "went underground." And to the dismay of the missionaries, they continued to hold their round dances and prairie chicken dances much as before. Pow-wows are still held throughout the summer months when Cree gather to cement kinship ties, engage in courtship, visit, exchange, and share the things that keep a people together. Now that the government ban on the Sun Dance has been lifted, this four-day ceremony (the number four is sacred in Cree beliefs) is a publicly proclaimed affair.

The Cree remain as sensitive as ever to the "sacred circle" of nature's seasons with its cycle of changes. Winter is a time for cutting wood and hauling it out of the bush, visiting by sleigh, playing hockey, hunting for extra food, holding indoor pow-wows, playing cards inside the house, and a host of other activities. When spring comes, the family pitches a tent to camp outdoors as in the old days; food is prepared on open fires and people sit outside to visit. Travelling to pow-wows and camping at them is common, with everyone relaxing and enjoying the outdoors. When fall comes there is hay to stook, wood to chop and stack for winter, crops to harvest, mud plastering to put on the sides of the log house for winter insulation, and all the other tasks associated with preparation for the coming of the cold months.

The Cree have always exhibited a well-developed artistic ability with a heritage of beautiful beadwork and quillwork embroidery in floral and geometric block design. While women were skilled in beadwork and quillwork, the men painted on buffalo hides to record their exploits for posterity. Some argue that Cree beadwork arts have reached new heights in the reserve period because now women are freed from many old tasks and can devote more time to these decorative crafts.

In the parklands of northwest Saskatchewan, around the historic communities of Battleford and North Battleford, are ten Indian reserves: Thunderchild, Moosomin, Little Pine, Lucky Man, Poundmaker, Sweetgrass, Onion Lake, Loon Lake, Mosquito/Grizzly Bear's Head, and Red Pheasant. These reserves are the home of about four thousand treaty Indians, most of whom are Cree. In addition, there is an equal number of Metis (or mixed-breeds) living at the fringes of both the reserves and the white population centres. On the Red Pheasant reserve, located some thirty miles south of North Battleford, was born Allen Sapp, a brilliant and fabulously gifted Cree painter.

Allen Sapp's Childhood

Maggie Soonias, the now-famous grandmother of many Sapp paintings, acted as midwife on the night of 2 January 1928, with the Nootokao assisting, when her daughter, Agnes Sapp, kneeled on the earth floor of the Soonias' log cabin, gripped the edge of a table and gave birth to her first son, Allen.

Albert Soonias and Alex Sapp, grandfather and father of the infant, kept clear of the cabin as they waited for the delivery. In earlier times, a volley of gunfire would have heralded the arrival of a firstborn son, but the old ways were going.

Alex and Agnes Sapp lived on the reserve adjacent to Agnes' mother and father. The original surname was Saposkum (He-passes-through), but it was anglicized to Sapp to help them fit better in the surrounding white world. The Sapps had seven children–Virginia, Julia, Allen, Simon, John, Stella, and Henry–but only Allen, Simon, and Stella lived to adulthood. During much of Allen's boyhood, his parents lived in a cabin next to Agnes' parents. Albert Soonias was a fairly prosperous Cree elder with more than 100 head of cattle and a good plot of land for the raising of hay. Maggie Soonias raised chickens, so the family was considerably better off than the average Cree, and there was plenty of work for the young son-in-law, Alex.

It is customary for Cree grandparents to take a strong role in the rearing of their grandchildren; for Albert and Maggie, lavishing care and love on their grandchildren was a necessity because of the ill health of Agnes Sapp. Even when Allen was born, Agnes had been afflicted with tuberculosis, and required periodic hospitalization throughout the 1930s. As a result of Agnes' frailty and the debilitating effects of the disease, her mother became much more than a "babysitter" to the children. It is natural, then, that Allen loved his grandmother very much and her life and activities became one of the most recurrent themes in his paintings.

Maggie Soonias was hard pressed to rear Allen to manhood, because he was such a weak and sickly child. Maggie was aided by her elder sister, the Nootokao (old lady or elder) who was wise in the ways of Cree religion and medicine. She was present at Allen's birth and had performed the traditional ritual of circling the building three times in order to win the blessing of the Cree spirits. Moreover, her knowledge of Cree medicine enabled her to make many potions, teas and drugs that helped Allen. The strength of her Cree faith and her knowledge of herbal medicines is possibly in large part responsible for Allen's survival through a difficult childhood.

It was also the Nootokao who gave Allen his Indian name. In the spring of 1936, when Allen was just eight, he was having another bout of very bad health. The Nootokao arrived, this time not to prepare the usual ginger root poultice and balsam fir tea for the ailing boy, but with a prediction, a warning. Her dream of the night before showed clearly that the child was in imminent danger of dying; and the Nootokao's dreams, the Red Pheasant folk believed, could be relied upon to predict events with startling accuracy.

When the children were asleep the Nootokao delivered her message to the parents, grandparents and several other adults crowded together in the cabin. Allen, she told them, firstborn son of Saposkum, would certainly die–unless a new name, an Indian name, were given. With the bestowal of that name, Allen would live long and prosperously. He would be a blessing both to Naheyow and the white race.

The Nootokao stood by Allen's bedside, touched his head and repeated in Cree: "This child is Kiskayetum" (He-perceives-it).

The matriach had taken upon herself the traditional right of a male elder of the Indian band, usually a close friend of the father. Nobody questioned her assumption of that right.

The sweetgrass ceremony, the simple observance that precedes or concludes almost every important occasion followed. The grandather cut four inches from a rope of pale green braided sweetgrass, sat crosslegged on the floor, then held a match to the loose ends of sweetgrass fibre. As the faint aroma filtered into the room, Albert Soonias intoned a prayer in Cree for the boy's safekeeping, health and longevity, and the same for all within the house.

Albert's long ceremonial pipe was removed from its cotton wrapping and filled with tobacco, and the men smoked in turn.

The elders respected the name change, but the younger generation took the name less seriously. They had, in fact, nicknames for the boy who had a dread, verging on terror, of the other children of Red Pheasant. One of his Cree acquaintances wrote:

> . . . Allen Sapp seemed to be a frightened little boy. He had to do what he was asked to do. If he was asked to dance a jig he would dance, for heavens know what the bigger boys would have done to him had he refused to dance. He was an out-cast who did not take part in any thing, ball, skating, etc.

But at eight years of age Allen was constantly drawing with bits of charcoal, with any stub that made a mark on wood or bark, leather or scraps of paper.

He never attended school for more than a few days at a time, and never learned to read and write but his teacher sometimes awarded his drawings as prizes to the other children.

During the winter months, whenever a visiting minister conducted a service at the little church of Red Pheasant, the grandparents wrapped the boy in blankets and bundled him into the cutter, for this was also a social event. But Allen never liked the white man's church service and was allowed to remain in the sleigh until the end of it. He was experiencing a gradual deepening of faith in his father's religion.

Alex has described these influences on his son:

This is the way it is when I come to see him, not to forget Manito. I told him-thank Manito, as you waken each morning. And think of him before you sleep. So he has reached as he moves about today.

Show you are of Naheyow, I told him-an Indian. I told him-let your hair grow, we are gifted to let our hair grow. It is like a burning brand on all of us.

I cannot talk too much on it, because I will talk too long. As you see him now, Ah!-from way out there, Little Pines Reserve, when night falls, burning incense of sweet grass aroma . . . In the mornings some times I sing in the mornings-thanking songs or chants of thanks.

I have pass-on those songs to him, to my son Allen. Those songs first, then Our Father, then Son of Manito or Son of God, then the spirits. I thank Him then for medicine herbs. I give thanks for them.

All those what we see, great area of plants, all of them are Naheyow medicine herbs, all what is connected to earth, and water.

This son of mine, Kiskayetum, that is how I teach him. I cannot talk too much on it. . . .

But the most profound influence on Kiskayetum Saposkum, and upon his paintings, was Maggie Soonias, his grandmother; and it is their relationship that answers the question frequently asked: Where did Allen Sapp, born just eleven years prior to World War II, see the scenes recorded in his paintings? It is a valid question, for the artist indeed paints from memory, and it can be answered only through tracing the daily activities of the Cree in the 'thirties and early 'forties.

The Cree people farmed without machinery long after most white farmers of Saskatchewan had semi-automated equipment. So the Sapp paintings show the simple manual chores of all Cree farmers that had remained unchanged for decades. The Cree women are represented by his many portrayals of his grandmother.

Maggie Soonias kept him near as she fed the chickens, milked the cows and assisted her husband at the butchering of a steer. What did it matter that the child would stand for half an hour gazing up into the foliage of a tree while others of his age played and fought. Maggie understood the odd one, and he was aware of and counted on her understanding.

Summer-and the tents went up, some of them beside the Cree log cabins, others out in the bush for shelter in the berry picking season. When Allen was big enough to grasp a pounding stone, he and his grandmother squatted on the ground, mashing the seeds of chokecherries, while the juicy pulp poured down over the flat rock into a piece of canvas. The thick mash, once a preservative in the making of pemmican, was still used with beef and moose meat.

Whenever a moose was brought home by the men, Allen assisted Maggie to cut the meat into narrow strips. Together they trimmed small trees, made racks and hung the meat to dry for several days in the sun. It was up to Allen to keep a good smoke fire going until the moose meat was ready for storing.

During the winter months Allen watched his grandmother weave rabbit robes–60 pelts required for a child's blanket. He had helped snare the animals and prepare the skins. They cut the pelts into two-inch strips, placed the skins in a water bucket, then stretched and wrapped the wet lengths of skin around willow branches. When the strips were fully dry he pulled them from the willow poles: white tubes of fur ready for weaving.

Alex Sapp refers to this period of his son's life:

> Sometimes he would do little drawings, drawing all sorts. And my children, those others, did not do that, only him. Kiskayetum was watching us, listening, fixing little things with his hands, drawing pictures on wrapping paper.
>
> All the time we tried to keep this child alive. We told him stories about Manito, how the seasons bring up what we need, one after another, the foods for us. First the goose berries. Then, it happens in the warm weather, like taking steps, step by step, the berries, cherries, seem to be taking turns, one after the other. Then strawberries, choke cherries, raspberries, toward the end. Manito arranged how foods must come and grow.
>
> All the time, all the time when he was a child, a tall boy, he was doing sketches and drawings. He was strong to have a try at it, to get by as artist.

By 1941, Allen, now a thirteen-year-old, was experienced in the planting and harvesting work of his people, and as he worked in the fields with the men, he was keenly aware of his surroundings, absorbing and subconsciously recording everything for his future work. When the mowing was done he helped transfer the team of horses to the rake, its steel teeth bent to a semi-circle. Rolling ahead of the gathering teeth, the hay was like a sinuous snake.

Albert, Allen and a neighbour, Nicotine, cut poplar during the winter months, and stacked it to dry throughout the summer. As the three woodcutters and their horses moved along the icy road that ran through the reservation, their sleigh runners squealing, plumes of smoke rose straight up from the protruding stovepipes of the Indian homes and some of the log dwellings were half-buried in snow.

The grandfather stands with the axe on his shoulder–unwittingly a subject for a future canvas: "Looking for a Log." He selects a tree which suits his purpose–large enough to be useful, small enough so that he and the others can drag it to the sleigh. Soon the tree falls and Allen trims off the branches. The trimmed trees are placed in piles for loading, the team hitched up and the heavy, butt ends of the poles loaded so that the slender tips protrude some ten to fifteen feet behind the sleigh.

"Bringing the Firewood Home"–the subject of a score of paintings–had its origins along this road where a young woodcutter ran behind the sleigh, weary but still observing the commonplace for future paintings.

Although Allen was reared by his grandparents, the Sapp and Soonias families visited back and forth, sometimes remaining together for weeks at a time. Allen was a tall boy at fourteen, the oldest surviving child of the family, and there were many times when Simon, John, Stella and Henry were left in his care.

Cree children, like the children of white pioneers, knew at an early age how to work and be useful. Allen Kiskayetum Saposkum and his brothers were sent out to hunt, trap and snare small game-porcupines, gophers, rabbits, prairie chickens-occasionally wolves and deer. These all provided food, and the children helped to skin and tan them. Pelts became caps, mitts, blankets, jackets; quills were used for decoration.

Sharing their work experience and visiting among themselves made up the social life of the Cree. Families helped each other on the land, shared tools and equipment and sometimes supplies and commodities. Denied all forms of comfort and luxury, enduring extremes of climate in winter and summer, Indians and their children were subjected to sharply heightened experiences of life. Severity was the common element. After seeing his sick mother once in Prince Albert Sanitorium, Allen Sapp no longer questioned her absence. He was fourteen and she thirty-four when she died of tuberculosis in the winter of 1942.

The following year Allen was stricken with spinal meningitis, an illness more severe than any previous ailment he had suffered, and one which his father has described:

> My son Allen was very sick. He was fifteen I think. I was living at Little Pines and I hear he is in North Battleford hospital. Oh! He was very sick. I do not know the kind of sickness. He had trouble with his spine, and it got to his head, and he was all the time there, at the hospital, sleeping. Weeks, for many weeks he could not move. . . .

Many months of convalescence were spent in the tiny Soonias cabin, much of it in the iron bedstead shown again and again on Sapp canvases.

By the time he was sixteen, Allen was able to again help his grandparents but there were changes. Albert Soonias, now in his sixties, had sharply reduced his herd, and both Sapp and Soonias families were on relief, which meant poverty and bare subsistence. In 1945, Allen's favourite brother, John, died of kidney tuberculosis at age thirteen.

The deaths in his immediate family, his own grave illness, the poverty, and the departure of friends to World War II, combined to make Allen want to leave the reserve and live in North Battleford. It would be over a decade before he could make the move.

As a child, Allen had travelled by wagon and team to Battleford and North Battleford, some forty miles to the north, but, as with most Cree, the area beyond the reserves was largely a mystery. With the war, many Cree soldiers travelled far and their horizons were broadened in all ways.

Not all Indians of that era accepted or even comprehended the federal government policy designed to integrate the Indians with white society-a distinct contrast to the nineteenth-century program of establishing Indians on reserves. While many Cree, young and old, strongly opposed integration and ridiculed those who tried to live like white people, Allen Sapp was determined to make his way in the white society. The white man had become for him a symbol of everything he aspired to: health and success, security and comfort-and above all, the means of earning a living as an artist.

The "Indian-to-white" transition was slow, almost imperceptible. From 1945 to 1960 Allen Sapp continued to live on the Soonias homestead. Shortly after his mother's death he met his future wife, Margaret Whitford Paskimin of Sweetgrass Reserve, a quiet, beautiful girl two years his senior. Her father had died of appendicitis shortly before her birth, leaving his widow, Rosa, and one son. (When war came, although not of legal age, he enlisted and was killed at Dieppe, aged seventeen.) Rosa remarried and bore nine children to her husband Moses Paskimin, and it was through Margaret's experience in assisting her mother with the care of the children that she became expert in leather and bead work and acquired the traditional household skills of Cree Indian women.

A fragmentary but succinct description of Allen's life and activities between 1945 and 1960 is contained in a letter from Red Pheasant Reserve:

> . . . When Allen's grandpa died, Allen kept with his grandma, in the old log shack. The grandma sold the cattle. But Allen kept the horses and chickens. Allen didn't have no income, he use to take wood to Cando, which is our home town, 12 miles from the reserve. I knew he sold pictures in Cando for $5.00 a piece sometimes $4.00. But he was shy when he carried them in the streets. And I knew when he use to go to the butcher shop and ask for scraps. In fact many times he went to the dump grounds. He use to get something outta there. . .
>
> He use to sell wood for $5.00 a load. Many times, 40 below zero, he had hard times. The same time he would snare rabbits. Also he use to cut willow pickets and sharpen them. We use to sell them pickets for 3 cents a piece. But mostly he traded it for food.
>
> In 1945 we went to work for white farmers, picking rocks, for about two months.
>
> The day Allen got married Eli Wuttunee from Red Pheasant hitched a team of horses on a stone boat to deliver Allen and Margaret to the day school for their wedding.
>
> There was no big party for them just another regular day. Today Allen laughs and tells of those days, without sorrow. . . .

In 1960 Allen and Margaret Sapp, like the majority of Red Pheasant Indians, were still on relief. Allen travelled to the Battlefords whenever a ride in one of the dilapidated cars was offered. Sometimes he hitchhiked. Rarely did he sell more than one or two paintings, his sole reason for the journeys.

By this time Allen had changed his appearance. His winter clothing was thin, worn, but obviously white man's, from the small fedora carefully placed over his brow to the polished black shoes. The neat, dark overcoat contrasted with the parkas other Indians wore, and heavy, dark-rimmed glasses added a stereotyped correctness.

In 1960 Margaret Sapp was confined for the fourth time to the Prince Albert Sanitorium with a lung ailment. It was there that David, the Sapp's only child, was born.

Allen's beloved grandmother, Maggie Soonias, had died the previous year, and it was because of these two events, a death and a birth, that Allen decided that it was time to move with his wife and child to North Battleford.

Allen Sapp-Artist

In 1961 Allen rented the upper storey of a humble North Battleford house. Although the amenities were minimal, it was only in hospitals up to now that the artist and his wife had been accustomed to such conveniences.

In this clean, little flat Allen set up an easel. His first studio was closet-like in size, lit only by a neon light; his only equipment was a few brushes and a muffin tin he used (and still uses) for a palette. It was here that he painted late into the night. By day he was a salesman, peddling in the streets and selling to storekeepers–when he had the courage to enter their shops.

Berryman's Hobby Shop not only sold his paintings, but Mrs. Berryman showed him how to mix colours and experiment with pastels. She sold one painting of his grandmother for $5.00: today it would fetch a four-figure price. Allen sometimes worked at the hobby shop and occasionally met there with others to receive some guidance from local artists.

From 1961 to 1966 Allen persistently clung to his concept of himself as an artist capable of providing sufficient income from his art to sustain his family, but he felt even less provident in the Battlefords than on the reserve. He was still on welfare with its low payments and the few sales of his paintings yielded only trifling sums. He began to paint what he thought the public might buy: "calendar art."

Stereotyped mountain goats, ice floes, oceans, ferny forests–none of which the artist had ever seen–appeared in his work. He sold paintings at the fairs, circuses and public celebrations that were held in the city and in the small towns along the North Saskatchewan River. He made little on-the-spot sketches of children for fifty cents apiece. But the peddling was day-to-day drudgery and he was not always welcome on the streets of the Battlefords. Once he was taken into custody by a constable and told that a charge of vagrancy might be laid. At the police station a group of officers gathered round the incoherent Cree; unable to explain himself, Allen removed the brown paper from his painting and showed it to them. The constable who arrested him finally understood Allen's situation and bought the painting for twenty-five dollars, possibly out of embarrassment.

On a winter morning in 1966, Sapp hesitantly entered the North Battleford Medical Clinic to try to sell a painting to one of the doctors. The doleful figure was familiar to Dr. Allan Gonor, the clinic's director, who recorded the meeting:

> I always remember Allen walking down the street carrying his brown paper parcel. I didn't know who he was or what was under the wrapping. He always wore the same kind of clothing, his frayed coat collar turned up, the little fedora. . . .
>
> Then one day he came into my clinic. This was the start of an association which changed Allen's life quite drastically, and certainly mine and my

family's. Allen unwrapped a fine piece of calendar art, but it was only a kind of illustration. It didn't take long to find out he was trying to paint what white people might like.

He didn't return again for several months. This time he brought a portrait of Chief Sam Swimmer. I bought it at once and gave him a little extra money for supplies. 'This is much better,' I told him. 'You should paint what you know. You're a Cree Indian. Could you paint a picture of your Indian reservation?'

For the next four days Allen brought a new picture into the clinic, each one painted the night before. I bought one every day, and kept on buying. His first is still one of my favourites–Red Pheasant Farmyard. Ruth [Gonor] and I commissioned him to do sketches of our three children.

I soon discovered that Allen had a total of two brushes and a few little bits of paint. This had to be remedied. He had no car, of course, and Ruth and I began to drive him out to the reservations north, south and west of the Battlefords. Allen and his wife began to visit us in our home–and this is how our association started.

Since Sapp was bringing in more paintings than the doctor could afford to purchase, Gonor devised a more sensible and commercial arrangement for marketing the artist's paintings. Smith Atimoyoo, then Director of the Battleford Indian and Metis Friendship Centre, acted as interpreter, and the three men discussed the plan at length. Allan Gonor offered to provide Allen Sapp with a monthly income and to try to find markets for his paintings. Allen would no longer take welfare payments and would concentrate on painting. Sapp was worried at foregoing welfare, but he agreed to the proposal.

In 1967 Ruth and Allan Gonor visited Montreal to seek advice from persons knowledgeable in the art world, and to find ways of selling the paintings which were now accumulating rapidly. A Montreal dealer was impressed and exhibited the paintings in March 1968. They sold rapidly.

The director of the Winnipeg Art Gallery, Dr. Ferdinand Eckhardt, suggested that Winona Mulcaster, an art professor at the University of Saskatchewan, might become Allen's adviser. Twice a month during the winter of 1967 Gonor drove Allen to Miss Mulcaster's studio on the outskirts of Saskatoon, a round-trip of about 172 miles. Because the artist has a slight speech impediment and speaks little English, communication was difficult at first, but through the rapport they established and by illustration, she successfully conveyed to him some of the subtleties of placement, perspective, technique, light, shade, space and related objects, as well as the need for both freedom and restraint.

In September thirty-five Sapp canvases were exhibited on the grounds of Winona Mulcaster's home. She later described the event in the Saskatoon Star-Phoenix:

> . . . The paintings were shown in the natural setting of grass and trees. . . .
> When rain threatened the paintings were moved to the shelter of a car port, and here more than a hundred people, over a three-hour period, viewed the work of a truly amazing Indian painter. People forgot the discomfort of wet and cold. . . .
> Allen Sapp's paintings talk about the life of an Indian reserve, not in

primitive but in intuitively organized, realistic terms. With remarkable observation they record the way it is, sometimes mean, sometimes sweet, but always with restraint, with freshness and complete honesty.

His paintings are marked by a very personal kind of realism that is the result of his total involvement with everything he paints-the people, the landscape, the animals-he knows and loves them.

A very remarkable technical skill in the handling of both oils and acrylic paint is evident. This is obviously not the untutored hand of some part-time painter, but the understanding work of a dedicated artist. . . .

Some will call his paintings illustration, and they are, but they do more than merely illustrate. They catch a mood, a feeling, a quality that sets them beyond mere illustration. The vibrant aliveness of winter, the subtle undertones of an autumn landscape, the sad calm of an Indian figure-these are the meanings of his paintings. . . .

This modest beginning sparked interest, but no one was prepared for the explosion of curiosity and enthusiasm that marked Allen Sapp's first major exhibition at Saskatoon's Mendel Art Gallery just seven months later when some 13,000 viewers passed through the gallery on an Easter weekend. Red stickers quickly appeared on the frames and at the conclusion of opening night, most of the sixty-one paintings in oil and acrylic had been sold.

Buyers and art collectors, who regularly attend the gallery exhibitions came, but so did the man-in-the-street-old and young-and it was they who responded most to the paintings: "Lots of Hay at Red Pheasant"; "Will be Dancing Soon"; "Bringing Water In a Cream Can"; "Fixing Old Fence"; "Chopping Down Trees"; "Fixing the Halter Shank."

Most people were carried back to some personal connection with the land in a vaguely defined past, and the paintings seemed to wipe away distinctions between white and Indian people. This, perhaps, is at the root of the appeal, success and possibly the artistry of the Allen Sapp canvases.

Allen and Margaret Sapp attended opening night, and were startled by the response. Several times the artist exclaimed, "People like my pictures. I'm happy about that."

In appearance neither Allen nor Margaret had yet abandoned their assumed "white" role, a necessary part, they believed, of success.

A grant from the Indian Affairs Branch arrived shortly after the Mendel exhibition, at a time when the Sapps had just bought their first North Battleford home, a five-room bungalow.

Margaret Sapp described the event:

We were very poor living here in Battleford. We had no furniture except for a few little things.

We moved into our new house one day, January first. We moved our blankets and suitcases. That was nearly all we had. We had a birthday party for Allen the next night, January the second, in the basement. And we had music on the tape recorder, Indian music.

We danced and we had a little bit to drink. I had one bottle of beer. I don't like it much. Allen didn't have any. Allen doesn't drink or smoke.

Next day we went shopping for furniture on Allen's birthday. We bought everything on sale, a stove for $199, a fridge for $199, chairs and table, two couches, a folding bed for Allen's room, all things for our house.

Allen is lucky.

After the Mendel exhibition Allen continued to produce so prolifically that Dr. Gonor found it necessary to call upon a friend, businessman William Baker, to negotiate with galleries and handle all business matters.

Between April 1969 and 1970 six successful exhibitions took place in Canada, California and England. The following year there were twelve exhibitions in such diverse regions as Alberta, British Columbia, Nova Scotia, and North Dakota.

For some time the artist feared to paint anything that might indicate poverty, or that might be offensive to his people–a torn blind, a broken window, a damaged farm implement. Dr. Gonor detected this reluctance and discussed it with the artist. Sapp's new confidence soon resulted in the honesty and candour evident in his portrayals of the farming peoples of Eagle Hills. His photographic memory was no longer frustrated by fear of painting scenes that some might consider disparaging to the Cree.

Except for a season of instruction from Winona Mulcaster, Allen Sapp declines to receive any formal kind of tuition. He shows no special interest in the art of the masters; as he puts it simply, he likes all art. It is natural that his approach to painting is realism or representationalism; natural in that all of his artistic models were realistic and representational. Thus, Allen prefers to paint stories and scenes as they occur in reality, although he adds a distinctive touch of mood and feeling to all of his canvases by using a slightly impressionistic technique.

Ever since white artists such as Carl Bodmer, George Catlin and Paul Kane visited the plains area in the 1830s and '40s, and the Indians saw their on-the-spot paintings, the painted art of plains Indians has become ever more realistic. As the Indians moved onto reserves, their arts became influenced by closer contact with the whites' newspapers, magazines, books and posters. In particular, the classic Western painting of artists like Charles M. Russell and Frederic Remington was a strong influence on budding plains artists, almost all of whom are men. What Allen did was to take the notion of "art for art's sake" from the white man and wed it to an imagination uniquely his own. In this way, Allen Sapp has put onto Canadian canvases images which are distinctively "Indian."

But his approach is not derived from American Indian art and is original to the Canadian plains. His work might be taken as the paradigm of the emerging "Northern Plains Indian School" of painting in Saskatchewan. In the United States there are two dominant "Traditional" schools of painting: the Santa Fe Studio style of the southwest, popular from the 1930s to the 1950s, and the Oklahoma style of the southern great plains region. Since 1960, the newly established Institute of American Indian Arts in Santa Fe, New Mexico, has developed a distinctive expressionistic style fostered by the success of the contemporary painter Fritz Scholder. Allen Sapp, however, was never familiar with any of these approaches and he and his Saskatchewan Cree colleagues worked out their style by themselves.

His art is also quite different from the modern work produced in British Columbia and in central Canada. On the west coast of British Columbia, a host of

Haida/Tsimshian/Gitksan/Niska/Kwakiutl/Nootka artists are producing original works almost totally based on traditional themes of mythological figures and totemic/crest designs that date back to antiquity. To the east of the prairies, especially in the Canadian Shield region of eastern Manitoba and western Ontario, another group of artists, led by Norval Morrisseau, produces almost surrealistic paintings inspired by the age-old legends of the Woodlands Cree and Ojibway. While Canada's Pacific Coast and Woodlands Indian painters are making significant contribution to modern art, their work is clearly different from that of their prairie colleagues.

The subject matter of Allen Sapp's work is usually the life of his family and the people of the reserves of the 1930s and 1940s, an era of Indian life which has many stories to tell. He finds uninteresting the present-day prefabricated Indian homes, which he refers to as "government houses." The people and the land are what he knows best and these are what he paints.

This reverence for the land and nature is a pervasive feature of his canvases. The art critic of the *Christian Science Monitor*, Diana Loercher, said of his paintings:

> . . . there is an atmosphere of stillness and timelessness and sensitivity to the nuances of nature–the texture of grass, the changes of the seasons, the shades of the sky all rendered in an almost Scandinavian palette of brown, blue, and white flecked with color. Mr. Sapp has great reverence for the land, a tradition in Indian religion, and derives much of his inspiration from nature. A radiant light permeates most of his paintings because of his worship of the sun which 'shines down on the world and gives light so that people can see.'

A glance at any of one of his paintings readily confirms this feature of his work.

When summer comes and the June Sun Dances take place, to be followed by the July and August pow-wows, Allen does very little painting, being too busy with these activities. His time to paint is during the long winter months and he is a nocturnal painter, often not beginning to paint until very late at night and laying down his brush only when the first rays of the sun begin to spread across the Saskatchewan sky. He does not paint in the field or on location because, as he says:

> I got pictures in my mind, I see wood lying in a field. Wood rotten, but still there. I make pictures like I remember. That wood was old sleigh runner. I know about that sleigh. I go along in that sleigh, horses pulling . . . pulling . . . just like that. I paint picture of old sleigh. Just like I remember, long time before government houses come. I was little then, little boy. I watched all the time. That's the way I paint.

Thus, from his prodigious memory of scenes and events, he draws accurate pictures for recording on canvas. He gives each painting a descriptive and evocative title from a memory such as : "Helping His Neighbour"; "Bringing in Some Wood"; "Fixing Front End of Sleigh"; "Albert Soonias' Cows"; "Charlie Bear's Place." He says, "I paint because I like to paint not because people pay money for my work. Money, we need it but it is people who are more important." He believes profoundly that "painting is a feeling, just like Indian music is a feeling," but acknowledges that "I have to work hard. I have to think here," he says tapping his temple, "before I can paint it."

A letter from Florence King, staff member of a Toronto fine arts gallery, describes Sapp's appearance at an exhibition:

It is opening night of his exhibition in 1971. The gallery is filled with elegantly dressed men and women, a flash of black-and-white as maids serve champagne. A few haughty doormen and attendants stand about, red stickers quickly appear on the various paintings–great expectations.

And into the midst of this assembly strolls a giant of a man, uneducated, self-taught . . . dressed in blue jeans, jacket, wide brimmed hat with feather. His hair is braided and tied with deerskin and a splendid bead necklace hangs around his neck.

He is shy, ill at ease, yet grave and dignified . . . a stoic, getting through this somehow, nodding seriously as people gather around him. His eyes shine, he is happy but uncomfortable. He wants it to be over. He wants to go home.

Allen Sapp didn't stay long and hardly spoke a word.

The businessman of the Sapp enterprises, William Baker, confirms this view of Allen:

He doesn't care much for attending shows and prefers to be home or on the reserve. Where I have committed his personal appearance at galleries for a few days, he invariably wants to go home the night of the show. He will stay for two days and I have learned that this is the extent of his being away. Luxury hotels mean nothing to him and he would just as soon sleep on the rug as in a bed, and he does this often.

At one of our exhibitions in Los Angeles, the year of the big earthquake, I found Allen glued to his TV set. When he saw me he said–"People are being killed and I want to go home!"

In his hotel room Allen places an eagle feather and braided sweetgrass on the dresser saying, "It brings home here."

There have been many exhibitions now and scores of newspaper articles. The Canadian Broadcasting Corporation made a colour documentary: *By Instinct An Artist*, and Sapp has appeared frequently on Canadian and American television and in National Film Board presentations. His canvas "Getting a Drink" was added to the Royal Trust centennial collection. In 1975 Allen was elected to the Royal Canadian Academy of Arts for his achievements in the visual arts.

All of this success has not changed Allen's basic values. He neither smokes nor drinks, and remains intensely religious and spiritual in his approach to life as a Naheyow. His home in a pleasant North Battleford residential district is simply furnished and he has not got caught up in the materialism of the white man. But he has a new automobile so that he can drive out to the reserves to visit his people.

He enjoys the Sun Dances and pow-wows of the reserves and is an excellent pow-wow dancer, owning several beadwork costumes, some made by his wife Margaret. The pow-wows and Sun Dances have often been the subjects of his paintings.

By 1970 Allen Sapp was totally changed in appearance, his "whiteman" era over, the supposed stigma of Indian-ness transformed to pride of ancestry. As he has recently said:

I'm proud of my braided hair. I would be very unhappy if I had to cut my hair and lose my braids. Even white people greet me on the street, saying "Hello" to me. Also, our own Naheyow elders, they like it. I enjoy the way I am. I go to pow-wows, it does not hurt my work, but it helps me.

I enjoy native dancing, dressing myself in Indian clothes. I try not to be shy in a pow-wow, to help my friends with their dances. So that they, too, be not ashamed they are Naheyow, and be proud of it. They should know that they were gifted and created with a clean way of living; very clean, we should not be ashamed. Some of our people are ashamed of our old people. They think our elders are too traditional. But that's not the way it should be. It is good to do something that the elders like. Like giving them tobacco, anywhere, any time, even on the sidewalk. To say "Hello" to them and chat or talk with them.

It is evident that Allen Sapp agrees with many Cree elders today who teach that Naheyow must revert to their religion if they hope to win the struggle for equality with the white man. This is a time when many peoples are searching for their roots, heritage and tradition in North America. Part of the significance of Allen Sapp is that he, too, is searching for self in his people's history.

In March of 1977 Allen and Margaret Sapp's only son, David, died at age seventeen. They have no other children. Several years ago Allen made this comment: "If you lose money you can get it again. If you lose people they don't come back any more."

What is Allen Sapp's position among his Canadian and international contemporaries? Although this is a question posterity must answer, curiously enough it is an issue that reviewers of the media have not discussed. The hundreds of articles about his exhibitions are either complimentary, flattering, or non-commital. All contain praise.

In his book *Portraits From the Plains*, Grant MacEwan, author and former lieutenant-governor of Alberta, has written:

> . . . Canada's Indians need help. That much has come to be recognized without debate. More autonomy, providing greater opportunity for self-determination, has to be one of the goals. But there are other objectives. Needed is an appreciation for the arts and skills of which many of them are capable. Allen Sapp helped to prove something important about his people.

In Edmonton, Alberta, viewers lined up for two city blocks in mid-winter, waiting for the opening of Allen Sapp exhibition of paintings. Why? With charm and disarming simplicity the Sapp paintings tell a universal story of people on the land. Nothing is contrived or falsified. There is in the subdued tones and shrouded figures a quiet serenity traditionally associated with pastoral life. Only the dark faces portray a kind of suffering that is without protest, that shadows a fatalistic acceptance familiar to people of the land everywhere, of this and every generation.

What may be significant to critics and viewers of the future is the fact that in the midst of twentieth-century artistic chaos a quiet Cree Indian emerged. Kiskayetum: He-perceives-it. Saposkum: He-passes-through.

A Cree Life

When the time came to butcher a cow we all pitched in and helped my grandfather. Even my grandmother, my two young brothers, Simon and John. We all went at it, there's lots to do. When somebody killed a deer he gave most of it away to folks on the reservation. Insides of that animal is good too, from cows, deer, sometimes moose, rabbits. Old people knows what to do with all the parts, not wasting any. Smoking the hide, stretching, scraping it, that's tanning. Deer horns – lots of things we made with deer horns. That time we butchered the cow we didn't eat outside. Sometimes in the bush cutting wood, lots of times we cooked rabbits, eating outside.

We used to have lots of deer. Dried deer meat good for making
pemmican. You have to put sugar with deer meat and rub it real hard
and get stone and bang the dry deer meat to make it that way.

*In the summer time, cabins were too hot and people would like
to stay in tents. The people didn't just live in the tents because
it was hot but because they enjoyed living in the tents. The willow
pickets on the wagon would be sold to the white people and they
would make fence posts. Sometimes we get lucky and sell for 10 ¢
a picket, but most of the time they only pay 5 ¢.*

*In wintertime horses were free and ran around. Only the horses
the man needed he kept in the barn. Sometimes he needed more
horses and he would go looking for them. In summer, horses
would be kept in corral as horses go away too far because they
like oats. The would find oats to eat and sometimes eat too
much and get sick.*

Life is in that tree. We are out in the forest working all day, lots of days in winter. Horses are hitched up nearby, waiting, munching on hay we brought along. I took off my parka and my grandfather too, chopping trees. Two, three, four of us together working, some days only two. Somebody always shoots a rabbit or some little animal if we're lucky – for lunch. With a 22-rifle.

I used to fill up a pail with snow and get the fire going, boiling the water over the fire for cooking the rabbit. It smells good cooking. My dog eats the insides. It is time to fill up the tea pail we brought along, fill it up with snow. We sit around on logs. It's nice there – some blue-colour birds around in winter, tatesew we call them.

The logs we took home – we laid it up all summer for good burning when the next winter comes. Wood cuts easier in winter.

Allen Sapp

*The feathers are used for pillow and also for mattress to put on
bed. Prairie chicken is nice for soup and also nice for eating.
Prairie chicken sometimes hard to find.*

Lots of work to do in summer. First the mowing. We sharpened up the mower knife on a big turnstone, John or me splashing water from an old tobacco tin. Two horses was hitched up, one of the men would do the driving, I drove the team when I was older, kids running behind. Little mice had nests there, as we mowed along we saw them running out all ways. Ducks' nests were hid there too, fox holes and hills the gophers made. Soon it was time for the raking if the weather was dry. We used to give the rake one family to the other, sharing that rake. It lifted a load when we pulled a handle, then dropped the load where we wanted. Stooking–sometimes Indian women came out to the field, helping with stooking.

*When I was little boy I went out sometimes with my
grandfather and Wuttunee to get a load of wood. In the bush
we cut the wood, we loaded it up on a sleigh and brought that
sleigh back home. Before I was artist full-time I used to cut
wood and sell it in Cando to get money, or trade the wood for
food for me and my family. Those were hard times, not
like today.*

People take along things for camp in cart pulled by horses. Canvas tent, pillows, blankets, suitcase, rope, big box of groceries, stove made from old wash tub to keep the tent warm and for cooking. They would take bannock and a 22 rifle to shoot rabbits and prairie chickens. They found water in sloughs. This road in Red Pheasant and leads to "Strawberry Town". Nobody knows why this name. The dogs would run under the cart on hot day to keep in the shade.

*My grandmother was all the time needing water for cooking,
washing up, doing all things she needs water. I and my
brothers, when they was there, even Stella and Henry, we
carry water from the slough, water from rain and snow. That
was clean water, we drank it when it was clean. Sometimes it
dried up in summertime, windy days, hot days, one after
the other.*

I was sitting by the table thinking what to draw, nobody around, me and my
grandmother alone in that place. She comes to my mind, the one who raised me.
I speak to her a little bit, ask her if it's okay to sketch her face. I never done that
before.

She says–"Yes, Grandson, that will be fine, while I am still here." My
grandmother was thinking about that too. "You can draw my face. It is not too
far off for me to be here no more." She tells me that, sitting very quiet. When I
finished I told her it was done. That was only a quick job. Later I done
a good job.

48

My grandfather had two, three stables for our cattle, big stables. Cattle was kept inside at nights when winter nights was very cold. It was a big job putting up enough hay for the winter. I helped with that.

I remember a cold winter day one time – Alex Nicotine borrowed the horse from his friend to go out there and find his own horses who wandered away. In my picture he found them. Alex will chase them back to his own home.

They put sticks together to make a stone boat. Not far from this place there used to be a well. They get water from well by putting pail into well and pulling it up and putting water into the barrel onto the stone boat and pull it.

A lot of Indians from many reserves come to the Battleford's Pow-wow. We put up our teepees and tents around the Big Top which is where the people dance. We also have seats for people and where the Indians dance to the sound of the drummers and singers. Now some of the Indians buy their drums. But in the old days they made them from moose hide. The older people pray and smoke a pipe before the start of the pow-wow. They do it before sunrise. Prizes are given to the best singers and dancers. Sometimes too for the best costume. No liquor is allowed but sometimes drunk people try to go there. But the police send them away.

Now some Indians bring their tape recorders. They do this to practise songs and dancing. Before the start of the pow-wow, we have a big parade through town to let the people know that the Big Top will be starting soon. People camp out here and they bring along rabbits, deer, and prairie chickens. Now a lot of them bring canned foods.

Pow-wow . . . people coming together, old ways again. It's hard to say-good to go back so young people can learn, so they won't get lost. Those kids learning from their folks. It's nice for mothers, fathers to speak to children, to rest, visit around. Men smoke a little bit, laugh, be happy together.

This is the only way people get to know each other from different places. Drummers take turn playing. Other drummers from different reserves also play. People bring tape recorders so kids can practise dancing at home. Older people teach younger people different dances so kids be happy about it. Different dances: chicken, owl, round dances and other kinds. Always dance the way the sun goes.

*In the old days we didn't have pow-wows. We called them sun
dances. People got together for sun dances, coming along in
their wagons and teams. Now people come in cars, trucks,
mostly old ones. We prayed to Manito at sun dances long ago.
We pray to Manito just the same at pow-wows.*

*The mother is looking after the baby. They wrapped the baby
in moss to keep it dry in the old days. The baby was tied in the
swing so it couldn't fall out. They used to put me in one of
those things when I was little. In those days babies didn't need
diapers. This was the way when I was born on the reserve.
The baby got food from his own mother then. He was too
young to get it from the cow.*

My grandmother used to make rabbit soup, good soup. Snares was what we used to catch rabbits, sometimes we'd go alone, sometimes we went with a bunch of children, all together, men and women, out to snare rabbits.

We pick a long, narrow bush and hang up snares on one end of the bush. Quiet, we was all pretty quiet. The men and children, very quick, make a lot of noise at the other end of the bush and come out running, scaring the rabbits along to the snares. Those women tap the rabbits on the head, taking them outta' the snares. Only a couple times I remember that. Mostly my grandma' and me snare rabbits alone.

This was another time for visiting after the preacher is finish talking, or before. Not the same preacher, another one come each time. Sometimes nobody comes for a long time, it is a long winter. Sometimes he was bringing some clothes for giving away, sharing clothes to Indian peoples. He come a long way on a cutter, only one horse. He tells the Indian people about Christ, Son of God. We know about God, about Manito. All things around us speaks about Manito. Hard to say-moon is working for God, the sun is a friend, everything with life is a friend. Nobody ever sees Him but there is God. There's no devil-lots of stories about a devil. There's no devil, no hell. Indians don't believe stories about that. That's what the White man teaches, not Indian people. God is in trees, the forest, all things with life. We believe that. There's only one God. The Wasayagak-we got stories about him. That's only for fun, for children.

Some people laugh at other people. They should laugh at themselves first – they forget to do that. When somebody says bad things people shouldn't fight back – just cut it, quick! Just sit and be quiet – be happy. If you lose money you can get it again. If you lose people they don't come back any more.

Somebody died in that house. In the old days my grandmother told me when she was a little girl they used to take the body out under their tent, first pulling out a couple of pegs. Never through the doorway. That was bad luck. Or if it was a house, the body was taken through the window. Somebody stayed by the grave all night before the funeral. That was the custom, not to leave the place with nobody around.

Things changed now. After the funeral friends go and visit the family where they lose somebody. They all sit on the floor. Some bring food. The elder in the family prays to God, he makes a pipe, three or four elders join him smoking. They eat food and pass it the same way the sun goes 'round. The old man in that family prays some more. Drinking tea at this meeting, no liquor. The women make some paper flowers for the grave and the Naheyow sprinkle little bits of things on the grave – bits of coloured glass, sometimes a toy or a doll. Sometimes a woman hangs up her praying beads on the grave if it has a cross.

Stove work pretty good. Nice to eat rabbit soup. Sometimes too
many mosquitoes and flies. Sometimes gets cold at night.
Had plenty of blankets to sleep on. Sometimes put cardboard
boxes on ground and put blankets on top. Makes it nicer to sleep.

We used to play hockey. But no skates. Only a few kids had skates, one or two kids. I made my own stick with hammer and nails. They all made them like that. Horse dung, frozen hard, we used that for a puck sometimes. We wore rubbers over our moccasins, too slippery for just moccasins or shoes. That was long time ago.

*Used to make rope from string to tie horse's legs together so
doesn't go too far. Sometimes used to put a bell on horse's neck.*

That train come from Regina, stopping at Cando about five miles from my reserve. My grandfather and some elders would meet the train. This time they are waiting to pick up some new clothes the government sends to chiefs and councillors on the reserve so they will have new clothes if they go to some big meeting. It is very cold, and they came down with horse and sleigh. That train will stop in North Battleford.

*Some people used to live there—Sam Nicotine, Charlie
Nicotine, Rayme Musak. We call that place Strawberry
Town on my reserve. Charlie Peychew he lived in a house to
the left that's outside my picture.*

On holidays or Christmas, people drove over to some friends to get food and drink together. Some singing songs and playing a drum in the house. Sometimes they drank whisky, if they had it, or made home brew. In the old days people never used to fight but now they do sometimes. The kids sometimes stayed home, looked after by the grandmother or some woman. Mostly they took the kids with them. Not many sleighs now, or horses. Some people working for government get new cars and sometimes some Indians have quarrels with other Indians. That is no good.

When I was little boy, my brothers and Stella and me, I remember we pulled a blanket over us in the sleigh, my father driving the team. Only my mother was away, she was in the san. That was Christmas day a long time ago.

*Going to make something out of it–axe handle. Lady got water
from well and just stopped for a moment to ask him what he
wants to eat.*

When I was a little boy I used to go swimming in the slough.
Other kids come too. Lots of fun. Sometimes we bring barrel
to get water. Wintertime chop ice so horses could have drink.

Mud used to fix house. Inside too, to keep warm. Put on fresh
every year so no frost gets inside. House real warm in winter time.
Log cabins real nice. Give nice feel.

*Talking only for a little while. Man going to take the wood to
white people's homes and sell it to buy meat or sometimes
trade for oats for their horses.*

*This is for two horses. Used to hook the wagon and the horses so
horses can pull wagon. Easy to make.*

People bring along lunches to the dance to use for eating later.
Sometimes dance stops and people eat together and then dance
again. Summertime they have pow-wow. Some people like
to visit and talk and don't dance. Lots of kids; but lots at home
with babysitter. After dance they give presents to visitors.

Use a lard pail for making tea. Also cook berries–saskatoons–
but first put in lard in frying pan. Sometimes if visitors came
we give them to eat together and talk and then happy. Always serve tea.
Tea is important for Indian people. My grandmother used to like so much tea.

*People liked to play this game especially at pow-wows. Hide
small stick in one hand and people other side guess which
hand. At this game people play drums and sometimes would
bet money. Sometimes also instead of money bet harnesses or
clothes. When person guess which hand the stick was in the
winner would then take over the stick, and the drum he would
give to one of the men on his side and they'd play the game the
same way as the other side. Lots of people would watch these
games and they would eat and watch at the same time.*

*Grandmother had lots of chickens. Liked to feed them. Had lots
of eggs so didn't have to go to store to buy them. Sometimes
sold some eggs, sometimes ate the chicken.*

Lady feeding the baby. That's the way it's supposed to be. Men will be home any time. Old lady is her mother. Likes to smoke a pipe.

*At the Soonias place–that's where my mother and father found
each other. I stayed with my Grandfather and Grandmother
Soonias. They wanted me there, like a son, their son. I wanted
to be living with my grandparents. My father didn't want me
to do that at first but my mother was sick and away at the san,
many times. That was my old place on Red Pheasant Reserve.*

The man is not home. He went to work for the white people. Lots of times used to have jobs from white people but not any more. Now he needs help as no jobs. Some say Indian people are lazy but not so. No jobs. They need help.

There's too much electricity now. We worked real hard before.
People gotta' work up a sweat, gotta' get the feel of what
they're doing. I work up a sweat painting at nights–two,
three, four, sometimes later in the morning when I quit. All
night sometimes–that's the way I work. If I got the feeling for
what I paint it goes alright. But I got to have the feeling to
paint the old people like I remember a long time ago.
Sometimes I sweat painting pictures at night.

If fire start to go out we'll have to go out and bring more wood inside. Sometimes we'd be very cold but have to go out anyway to get it.

People liked to get together–sew together. That's nicer that way.
Always have tea when get together.

People met on the road and talk. Mostly looking for jumping deer but just get rabbits or prairie chicken sometimes. People on sled say farmer coming to buy wood off them tomorrow. And other man tells them to ask farmer if he needs more. He has some. Helping each other.

That's all for the day. Have been working hard today. Now going to go home and rest. Have to walk to warm up.

*My grandmother's brother used to keep horses there when he had
them. He had a wagon. Used to drive around the reserve.*

I went there as a kid. Mostly I draw cowboys and other kids like my drawings. Instead of making letters I was drawing pictures. The teacher came and gave me heck.

Seneca root used for medicine. White people used to buy it to make something out of it. Seneca root sometimes hard to find.

Selected Bibliography

Ahenakew, Edward. *Voices of the Plains Cree*. Edited by Ruth Buck. Toronto: McClelland & Stewart, Ltd., 1973

Bloomfield, L. *Sacred Stories of the Sweetgrass Cree*. Ottawa: National Museums of Canada, Bulletin no. 60, Anthropological Series no. 11, 1930.

Bradshaw, Thecla (Zeeh). *Recent Paintings by Allen Sapp*. Exhibition Catalogue. Saskatoon: Mendel Gallery, 1969.

————"Spokesmen for White and Indian," *The Indian Record*, vol. 37, nos. 1/2, 1974.

————"A Thousand Paths to Choose," *The Northian*, vol. 6, no. 1, 1969.

Cardinal, Harold. *The Unjust Society*. Edmonton: M. G. Hurtig, Ltd., 1969.

Dickason, Olive Patricia. *Indian Arts in Canada*. Ottawa: Information Canada, 1972.

Frideres, James S. *Canada's Indians: Contemporary Conflicts*. Scarborough, Ontario: Prentice-Hall of Canada, Ltd., 1974.

Fry, Allen. *How a People Die*. Toronto: Doubleday, 1972.

Hickman, James. "The Quiet Birth of the New Indian Art." *Imperial Oil Review*, no. 2, 1975.

Jefferson, Robert. *Fifty Years on the Saskatchewan*. Battleford, Saskatchewan: Canadian North-West Historical Society Publications, vol. 1, no. 5, 1929.

Jenness, Diamond. *The Indians of Canada*. Ottawa: National Museums of Canada, Bulletin no. 65, 1932.

Johnson, Michael G. "Decorative Art of the Plains Cree and their Neighbours." *American Indian Crafts & Culture*, vol. 8, nos. 4/5/6, 1974.

Lovoos, Janice. "Allen Sapp, Cree Indian Artist." *Southwest Art*, vol. 4, no. 7, 1975.

MacEwan, Grant. *Portraits from the Plains*. Toronto: McGraw-Hill Co. of Canada, Ltd., 1971.

Mandelbaum, David G. *The Plains Cree*. New York: American Museum of Natural History. Anthropological Papers, vol. 37, part 2, 1940.

Musée De L'Homme. *Masterpieces of Indian and Eskimo Art from Canada*. Paris: Société des Amis du Musée de l'Homme, 1969.

Patterson, E. Palmer. *The Canadian Indian: A History Since 1500*. Toronto: Collier-Macmillan of Canada, Ltd., 1972.

Patterson, Nancy-Lou. *Canadian Native Art: Arts and Crafts of The Canadian Indians and Eskimos*. Toronto: Collier-Macmillan of Canada, Ltd., 1973.

Ray, Arthur J. *Indians in the Fur Trade*. Toronto: University of Toronto Press, 1974.

Robertson, Heather. *Reservations Are for Indians*. Toronto: James, Lewis & Samuel, 1970.

Skinner, Alanson. "Notes on the Plains Cree." *American Anthropologist*, vol. 16, 1914.

Towards a New Past. Saskatchewan, Dept. of Culture and Youth, Regina, Saskatchewan, 1975.

Warner, John Anson. "Allen Sapp, Cree Painter." *American Indian Art*, vol. 2, no. 1, 1976.

———"The Cree Artist Allen Sapp." *The Beaver*, Winter, 1973.

———*The Life and Art of the North American Indian*. London: The Hamlyn Publishing Group, 1975.

Major Exhibitions of Allen Sapp

1968

February	Eaton's Art Gallery, Montreal, Quebec
September	Winona Mulcaster's Home, Saskatoon, Saskatchewan
October	Teacher's College, Saskatoon, Saskatchewan
November	Marquis Hall, University of Saskatchewan, Saskatoon, Saskatchewan
December	St. Thomas Moore College, University of Saskatchewan, Saskatoon, Saskatchewan

1969

April	Mendel Art Gallery, Saskatoon, Saskatchewan
October	Robertson Art Gallery, Ottawa, Ontario
November	Zachary Waller Gallery, Los Angeles, California

1970

January	Alwin Gallery, London, England
March	Saskatchewan Power Corporation Building Gallery, Regina, Saskatchewan
April	Moose Jaw Art Museum, Moose Jaw, Saskatchewan
	The Gainsborough Galleries, Calgary, Alberta
June	Mendel Art Gallery, Saskatoon, Saskatchewan
	International Music Camp, Bottineau, North Dakota
	Alex Fraser Galleries, Vancouver, British Columbia
July	New Brunswick Museum, St. John's, New Brunswick
November	Centennial Art Gallery, Halifax, Nova Scotia
October	Upstairs Gallery, Winnipeg, Manitoba

1971

February	Memorial University Art Gallery, St. John's, Newfoundland
	Langara Gardens, Vancouver, British Columbia
	Zachary Waller Gallery, Los Angeles, California
March	Robertson Art Gallery, Ottawa, Ontario
April	Alwin Gallery, London, England
May	Downstairs Gallery, Edmonton, Alberta
August	The Print Gallery, Victoria, British Columbia
September	Gallery of the Golden Key, Vancouver, British Columbia
November	St. John's Ravenscourt School, Fort Garry, Manitoba
	Damkjar-Burton Gallery, Hamilton, Ontario
	The Sonneck Gallery, Kitchener, Ontario
	Downstairs Gallery, Edmonton, Alberta

1972

March	Damkjar-Burton Galleries, Hamilton, Ontario
	Downstairs Gallery, Edmonton, Alberta
April	Eaton's Art Gallery, Toronto, Ontario
	The Gainsborough Galleries, Calgary, Alberta
July	Alwin Gallery, London, England
September	Gallery of the Golden Key, Vancouver, British Columbia
	Eaton's Art Gallery, Montreal, Quebec
October	Downstairs Gallery, Edmonton, Alberta

1973

March	Eaton's Art Gallery, Toronto, Ontario
September	Gallery of the Golden Key, Vancouver, British Columbia
October	Downstairs Gallery, Edmonton, Alberta
November	Eaton's Art Gallery, Toronto, Ontario

1974

March	Alwin Gallery, London, England
April	Zachary Waller Gallery, Los Angeles, California
September	de Vooght Galleries, Vancouver, British Columbia
October	Continental Galleries, Montreal, Quebec
November	Downstairs Gallery, Edmonton, Alberta

1975

February	Eaton's Art Gallery, Toronto, Ontario
May	The Gainsborough Galleries, Calgary, Alberta
November	de Vooght Galleries, Vancouver, British Columbia

1976

April	Hammer Gallery, New York, New York
May	Edmonton Art Mart, Edmonton, Alberta
July	Rowe House Gallery, Washington, D.C.
October	Eaton's Art Gallery, Toronto, Ontario
November	de Vooght Galleries, Vancouver, British Columbia

1977

March	The Gainsborough Galleries, Calgary, Alberta
October	Continental Galleries, Montreal, Quebec
	Edmonton Art Mart, Edmonton, Alberta
	de Vooght Galleries, Vancouver, British Columbia

List of Paintings

A Cree Life: The Art of Allen Sapp

DESIGN AND PRODUCTION BY
David Shaw & Associates Ltd.

TYPESETTING BY
Compeer Typographic Services Ltd.

FILM PREPARATION BY
Herzig-Somerville Ltd.

PRINTED AND BOUND BY
The Hunter Rose Company Ltd.